Kemptville Ontario and Area in Colour Photos, Saving Our History One Photo at a Time

Photography
by Barbara Raué
2016

Series Name:
Cruising Ontario

Book 153: Kemptville and Area

Cover photo: 220-222 Prescott Street, Kemptville, Page 26

Series Name: Cruising Ontario
Saving Our History One Photo at a Time
in colour photos

Books Available in Alphabetical Order:
Aberfoyle, Acton, Alton, Amherstburg, Ancaster, Arthur, Aylmer, Ayr, Bloomingdale, Brantford, Burlington, Caledon, Caledonia, Cambridge, Clifford, Conestogo, Delhi, Dorchester to Aylmer, Drayton, Drumbo, Dundas, Eden Mills, Elmira, Elora, Essex, Fergus, Guelph, Hagersville, Hamilton, Hanover, Harriston, Hespeler, Jarvis, Kingston, Kingsville, Kitchener, Linwood, Listowel, London, Lucknow, Mono, Mount Forest, Neustadt, New Hamburg, Niagara-on-the-Lake, Oakville, Orangeville, Orillia, Owen Sound, Palmerston, Peterborough, Petrolia, Port Elgin, Preston, Rockwood, Sarnia, Seaforth, Sheffield, Shelburne, Simcoe, Southampton, St. Jacobs, St. Marys, St. Thomas, Stoney Creek, Stratford, Thamesford, Tillsonburg, Waterdown, Waterford, Waterloo, Welland, Wellesley, Windsor, Wingham, Woodstock

Book 114-116: Waterloo updated
Book 117-119: Windsor
Book 120-121: Amherstburg
Book 122: Essex
Book 123-124: Kingsville
Book 125-127: Woodstock
Book 128: Thamesford
Book 129-132: St. Marys
Book 133-136: Sarnia
Book 137: Petrolia
Book 138-139: Welland
Book 140-145: Kingston
Book 146-149: Ottawa
Book 150-151: Midland

Book 152: Penetanguishene
Book 153: Kemptville
Book 154: Cornwall
Book 155: Mariatown to Maitland
Book 156: Morrisburg

Other Books by Barbara Raue

Coins of Gold

Arrows, Indians and Love

The Life and Times of Barbara
Volume 1: Inventions That Have Enhanced My Life
Volume 2: Entertainment That I Have Enjoyed
Volume 3: East Coast Trips
Volume 4: Olympics Have Always Intrigued Me
Volume 5: Wonders of the World
Volume 6: Caribbean Cruises We Have Enjoyed
Volume 7: Animals
Volume 8: Storms and Other Major Disasters in My Lifetime
Volume 9: Wars, Terrorist Attacks and Major Disasters

The Cromwell Family Book

Laura Secord Discovered

Daddy Where Are You?

Montana Series
Book 1: Montana Dream
Book 2: Life on the Montana Frontier
Book 3: Montana to Boston and Back

Visit Barbara's website to view all of her books
http://barbararaue.ca

Table of Contents

Kemptville is a community located in south eastern Ontario in the northernmost part of the United Counties of Leeds and Grenville and is about fifty-six kilometres south of Ottawa. Kemptville Creek begins southwest of the town, divides Kemptville, and flows four kilometres to empty into the Rideau River. Kemptville is composed of forests and farmland. The name Kemptville was adopted in 1829 as a tribute to Sir James Kempt, the Governor of British North America.

In 1812, Lyman Clothier bought one hundred acres of land from John Byce for the price of a yoke of oxen, and a flintlock rifle. Mr. Clothier had lived in the area since 1804 or 1805, and in 1812 he and his four sons built a saw mill, and two houses in what is now Kemptville. The mill was important for the settling of the community; in order to construct a crude dwelling, lumber was required. The mill provided lumber for settlers throughout Oxford Township.

The village was located on the Ottawa-Prescott Road and many travellers passed through the settlement. One of Mr. Clothier's sons, Asa, opened his home to these travellers as a resting and meeting place. The "Clothier's Hotel" was born. A grist mill was added in 1821 when the Clothiers placed some grinding stones in the lower part of their saw mill. Rather than taking their grain to a site on the St. Lawrence River, a daunting hike in the best of conditions, the settlers could now take it to this grist mill. A blacksmith's shop was built and run by the Clothiers. A schoolhouse was built in 1823 and served the surrounding communities for many years. The first doctor arrived in the community in 1824. A weekly newspaper is published in Kemptville, called the *Kemptville Advance*, and has been published since 1855.

At least 10,000 citizens from the thirteen British colonies decided to remain as British citizens after the 1776 revolution. These loyalists and ministers of various faiths, who were generally attached to the army garrisons, came to Quebec and Nova Scotia after the revolution and were known as United Empire Loyalists. In 1784 several from the Montreal area migrated by bateau up the St. Lawrence River and settled in the area from the provincial line east of Cornwall to the Bay of Quinte.

Elizabethtown-Kitley is a township in eastern Ontario in the United Counties of Leeds and Grenville. Its southern border lies along the St. Lawrence River and it extends north into many rural hamlets and villages. Also in the township are Addison, Forthton, and Newbliss.

Newbliss was settled mostly by Loyalists or immigrants from the British Isles who received their land here as grants from the Crown. One of the first businesses to operate here was Dack's Tavern, built in 1817 and established as a tavern around the 1830s. The tavern had five rooms, three bed and horse stables, and also hosted Orange Lodge meetings. By the mid-1800s, the village began to flourish when roads improved in the area. By this time, the settlement consisted of two hotels, a blacksmith shop, a wagon shop, a general store, a post office, and its own schoolhouse. A cheese factory consisting of three buildings operated from Newbliss. The main building was later turned into the general store.

Kemptville

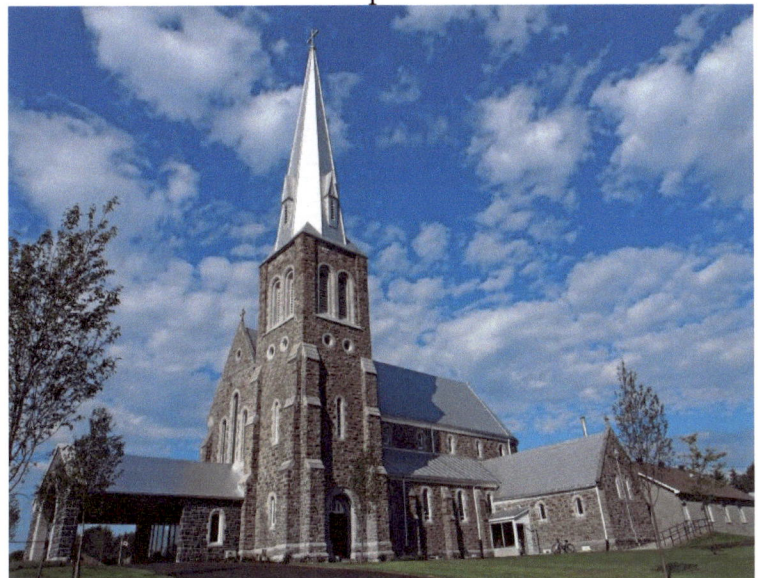

The Church of St. James the Apostle is located in the heart of Kemptville. St. James started as a mission parish in the Rideau townships in 1826. It quickly evolved into an Anglican parish, first as a frame building in 1827 and then in the current structure in 1878. The interior of the building is lath and plaster. Stencils in the ceiling of the nave represent the twelve apostles. One large stencil serves as the backdrop to the font. The alpha and omega stencils repeat the theme of the triptych window above the altar.

The stained-glass windows in the church are memorials to past members, early and late. They tell the history of the church. Each speaks of the mystery and joy of Christ and of our commissioning to be Christ's ministers and disciples. The oldest is the Stannage triptych, a memorial to the rector who died in 1880. On the west wall is the rose window, which was a gift from the children and teachers of the Sunday School in 1882. The tower bell from the 1826 church, though cracked since 1878, calls Anglicans to worship on Sundays, and tolls for members' weddings and funerals.

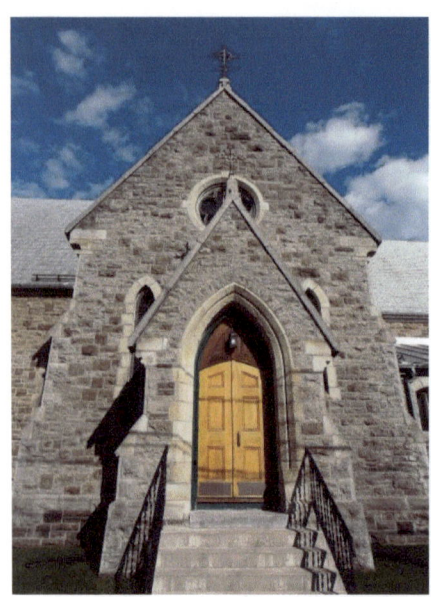 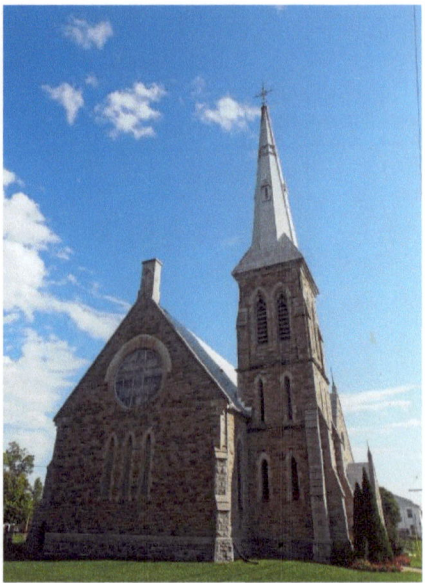

35 Clothier Street West – St. James Anglican Church - blue limestone – ecclesiastical Gothic architecture – lancet windows, buttresses, rose window, trefoil decoration on the tower

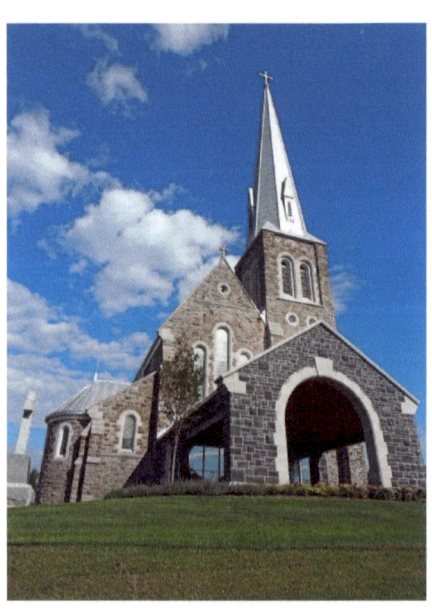

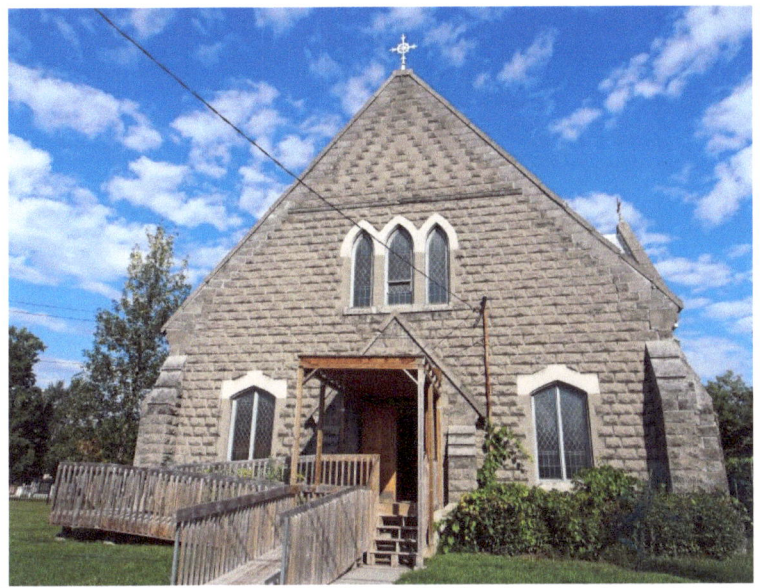

Clothier Street West – 1907 - Leslie Hall – for Sunday School and concerts

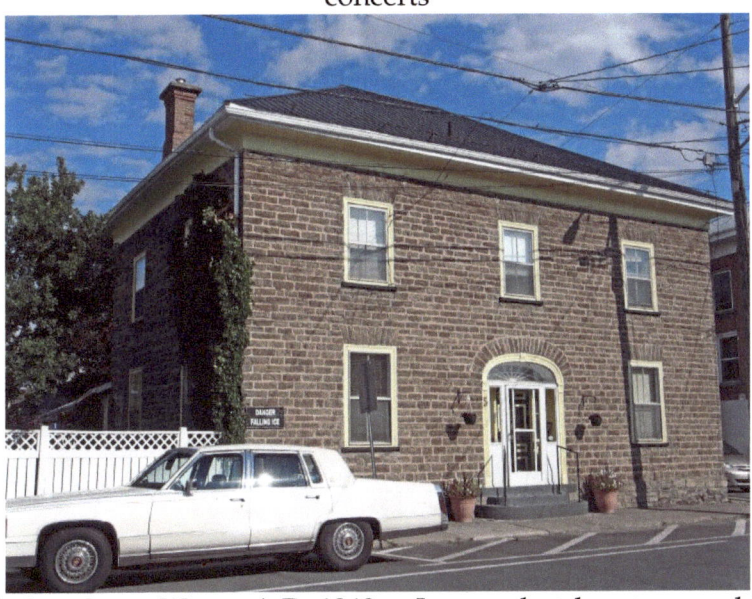

5 Clothier Street West – A.D. 1840s – It was a hotel, a store, and then a ladies' finishing school. Elizabeth Bell married Dr. C. F. Ferguson and moved into the house in 1897. – Hipped roof, voussoirs over door and windows

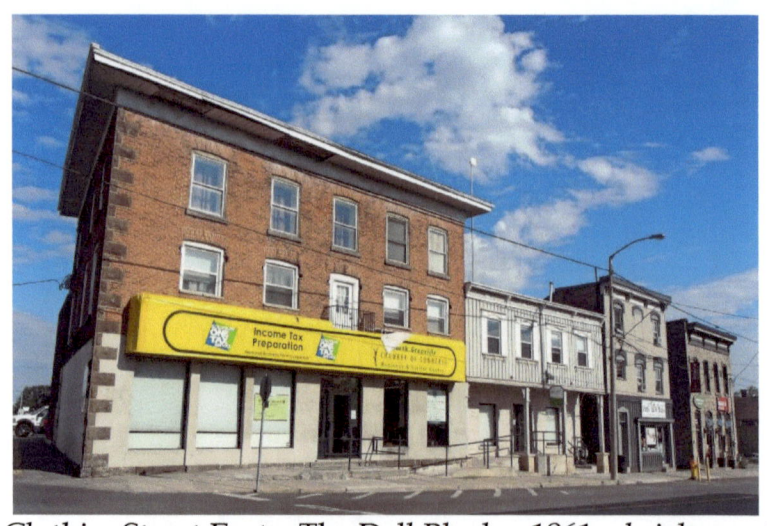

3 Clothier Street East – The Dell Block – 1861 – bricks made from clay taken from the river bank – corner quoins

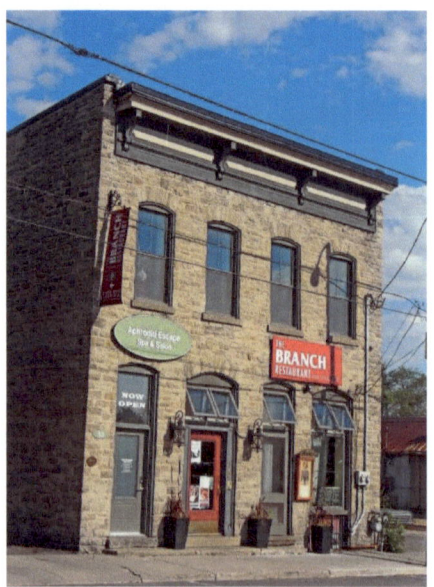

13 Clothier Street West – 1880 – Aphrodite Spa;
15 Clothier Street – The Branch Restaurant – cornice brackets

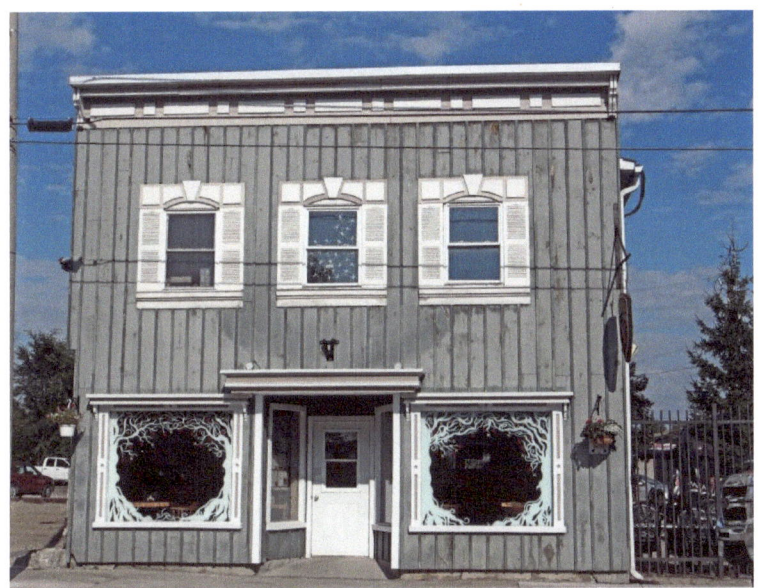

Clothier Street East - keystones

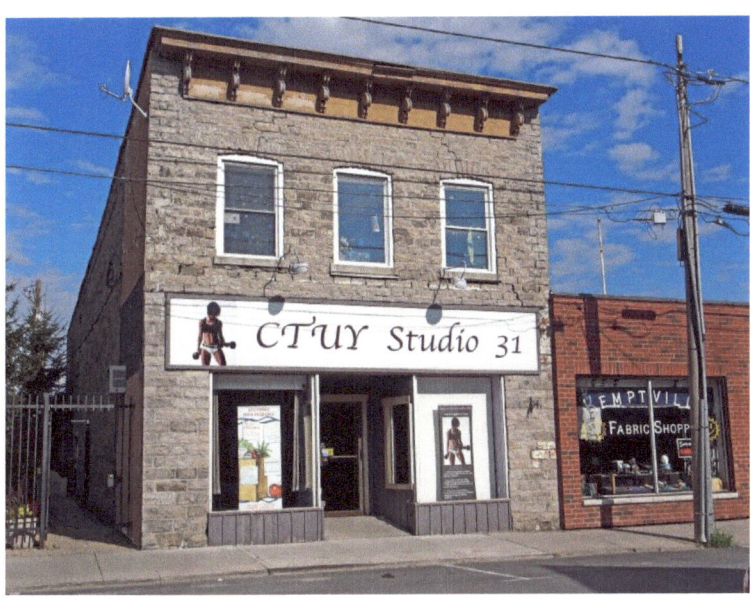

31 Clothier Street East – 1872 – cornice brackets

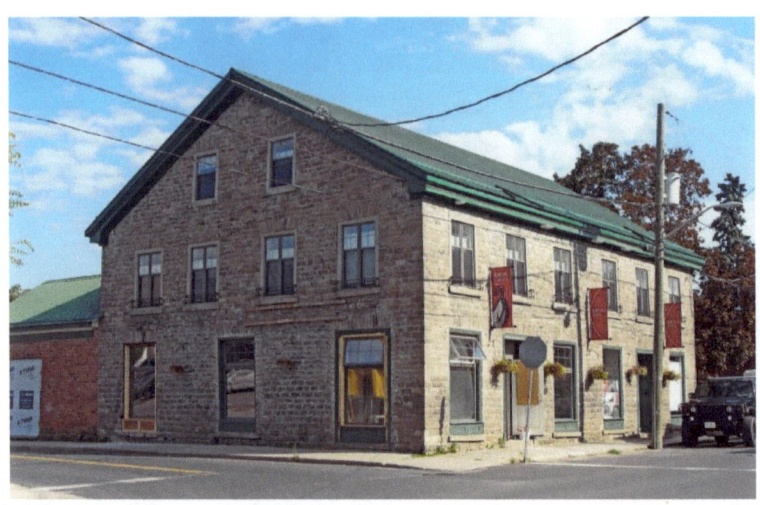

103 Clothier Street East – built in 1847 by Francis Jones, Land Surveyor and Member of Parliament from 1862-1874. General and furniture stores and undertakers have operated in the building, as well as the first newspaper.

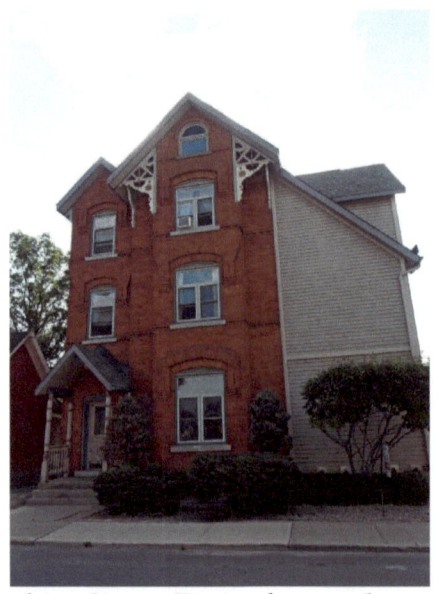

104 Clothier Street East – fretwork, voussoirs

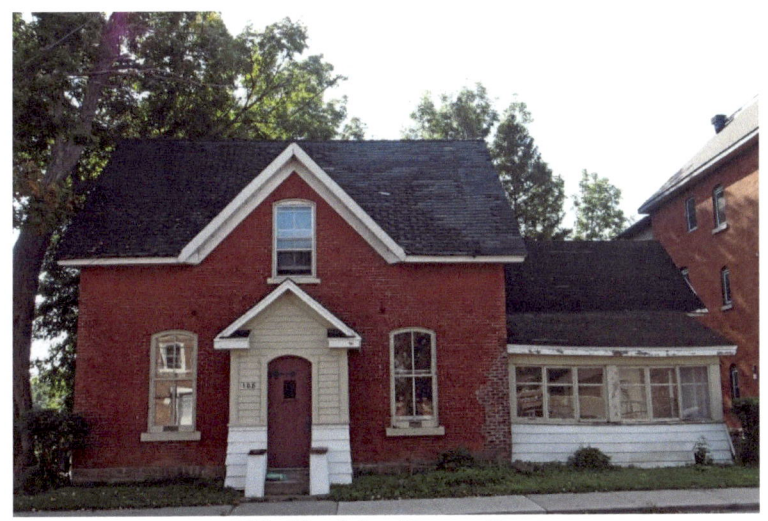

108 Clothier Street East

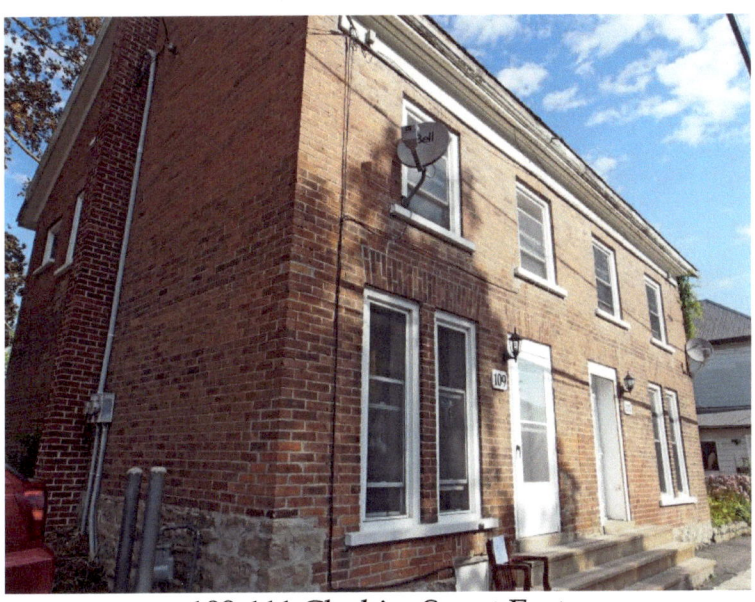

109-111 Clothier Street East

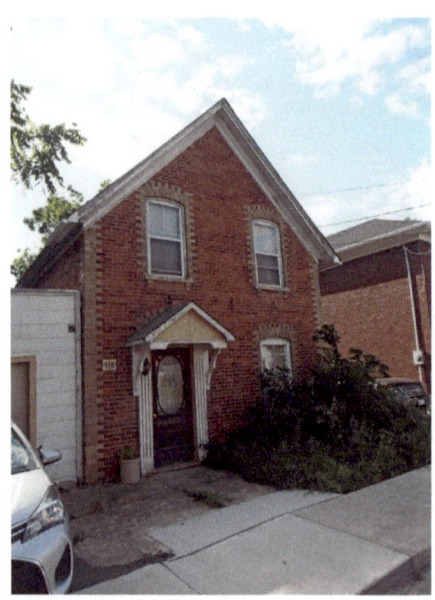

118 Clothier Street East – corner quoins

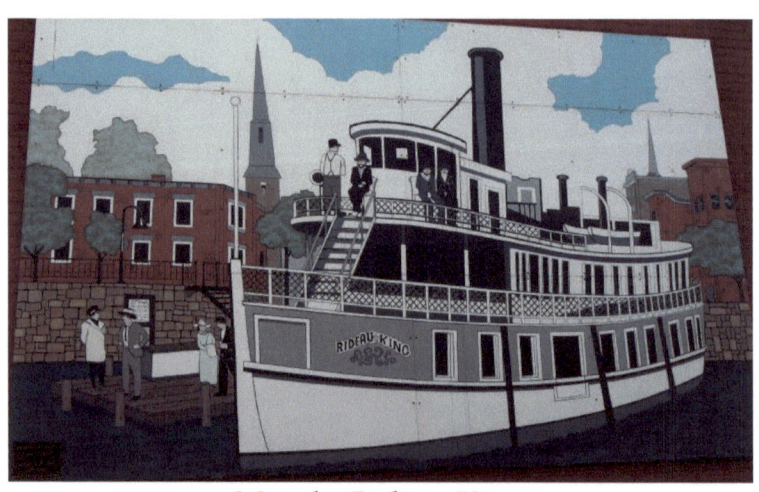

Mural – Rideau King

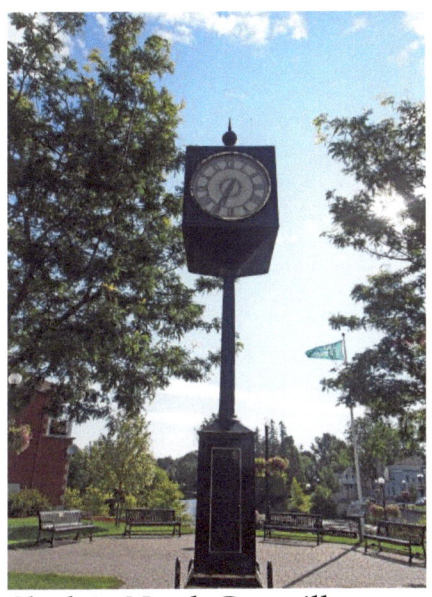

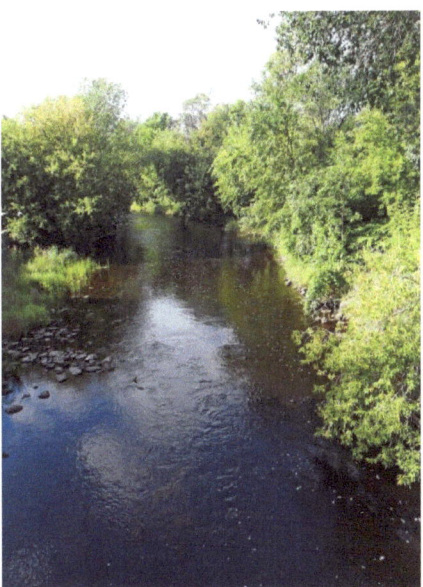

Clock in North Grenville
Rotary Millennium Park

Kemptville Creek

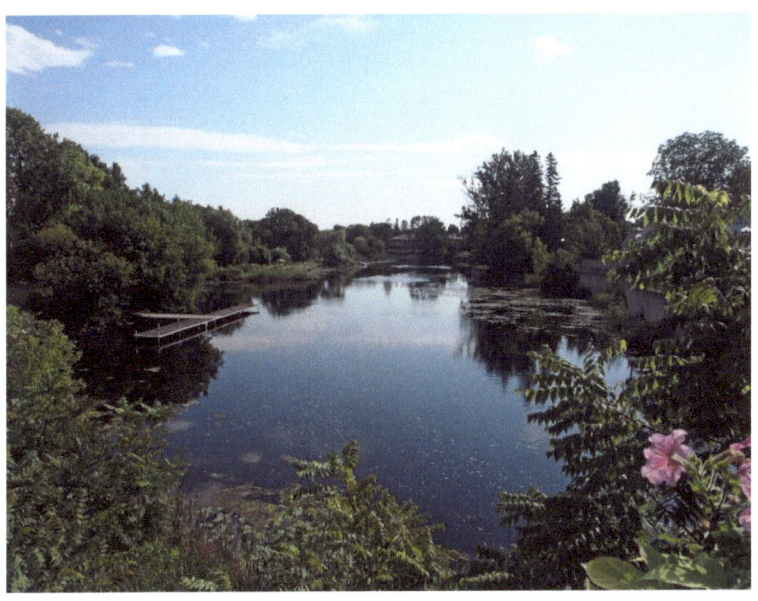

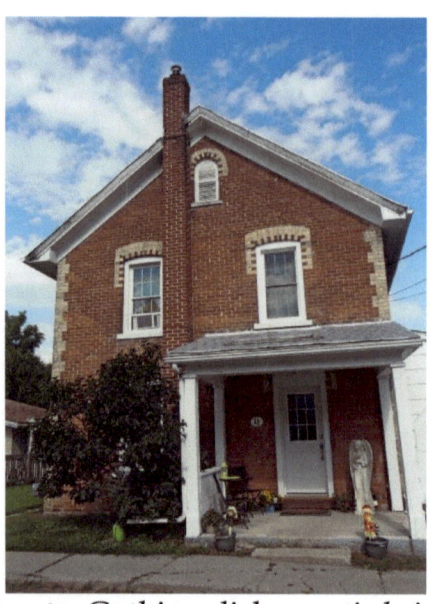

11 Elizabeth Street – Gothic – dichromatic brickwork, corner quoins

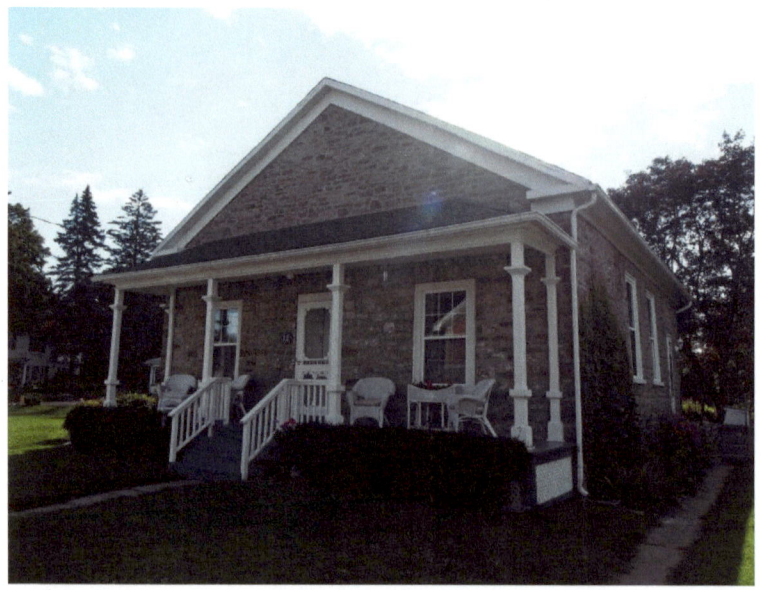

12 Elizabeth Street – Regency Cottage – gabled roof, open railing

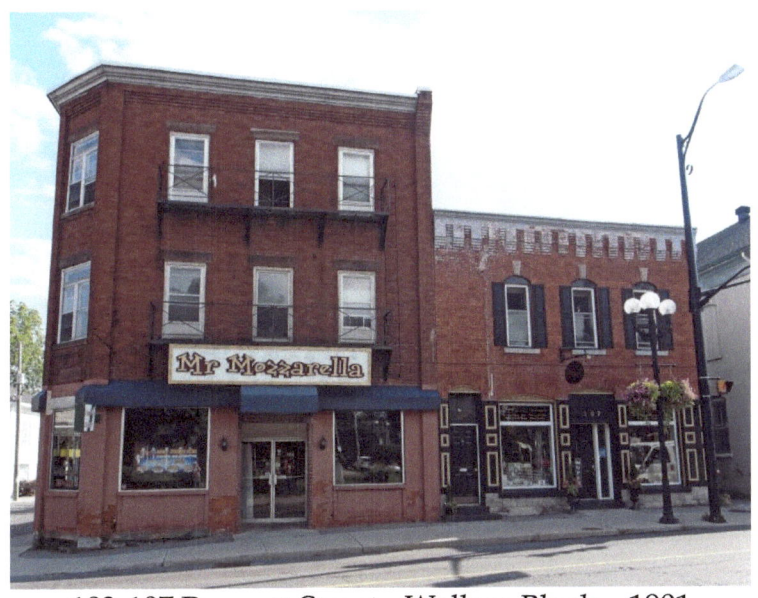

103-107 Prescott Street - Wallace Block – 1901
- voussoirs, keystones

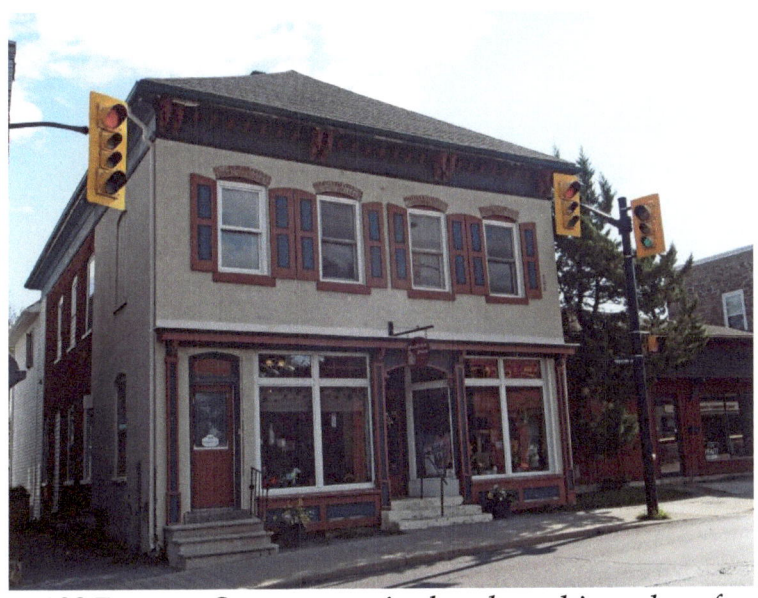

109 Prescott Street – cornice brackets, hipped roof

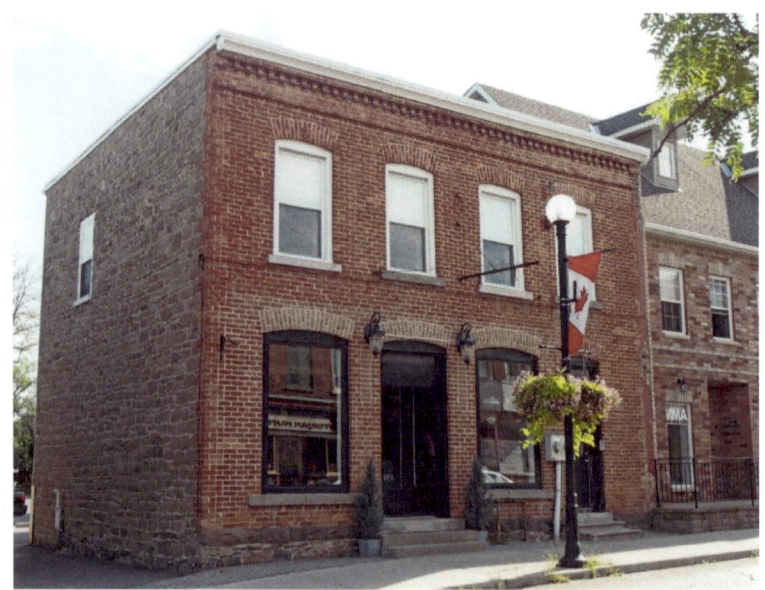

Prescott Street – dentil moulding, voussoirs

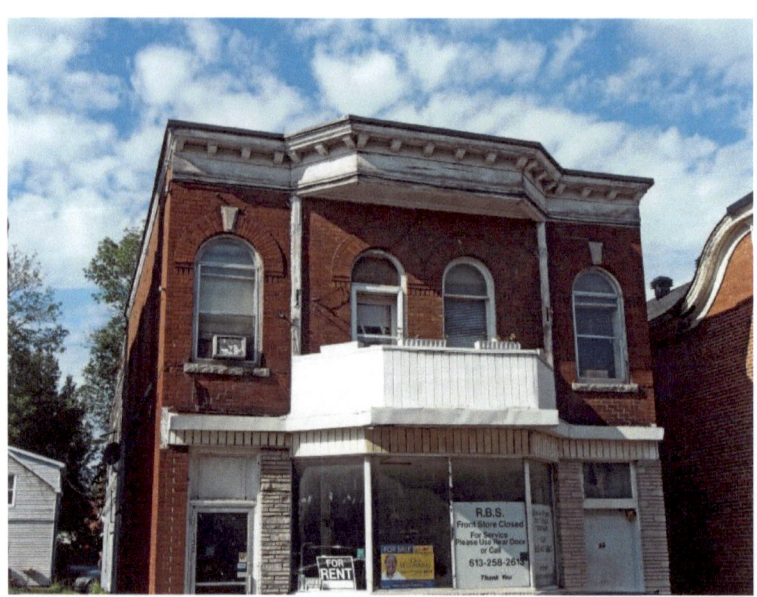

130-132 Prescott Street – cornice brackets, second floor closed
balcony, voussoirs and keystones

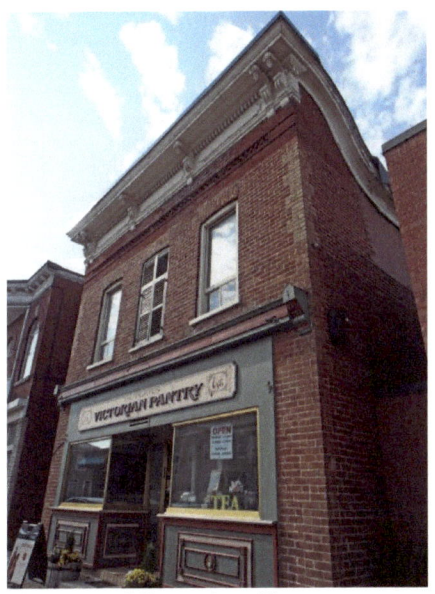

126 Prescott Street – Victorian Pantry tea room – 1872 -
William H. Cochrane opened a harness and saddlery business
on this site, complete with a manufacturing section and store.

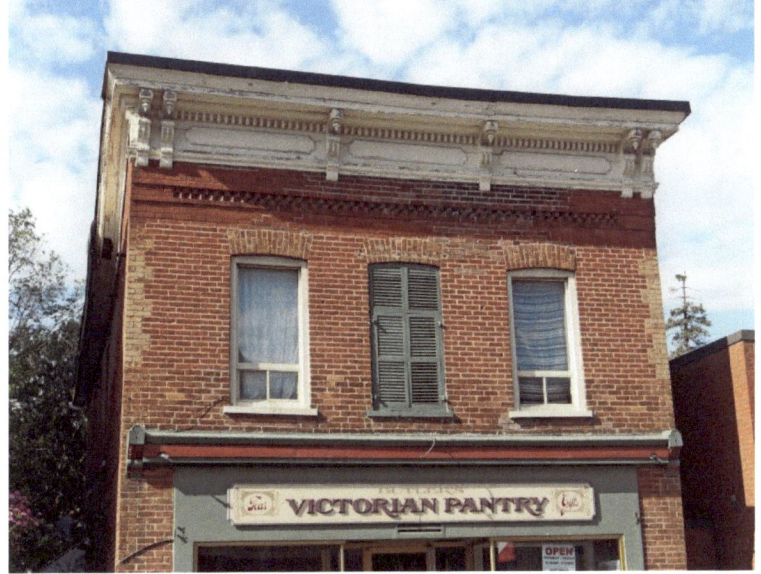

Cornice brackets, dentil moulding, corner quoins

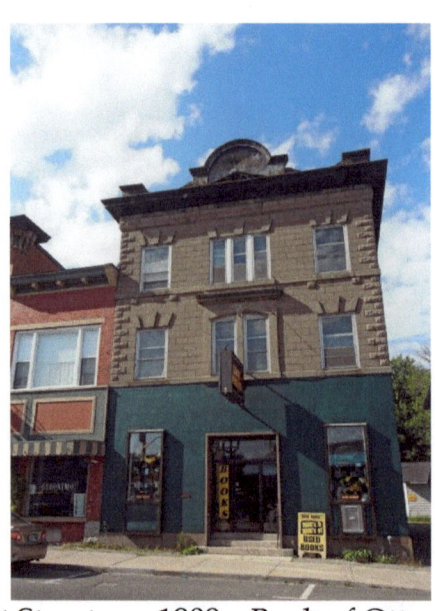

144 Prescott Street – c. 1909 – Bank of Ottawa used this location; amalgamated with the Bank of Nova Scotia and remained on the site until 1978; now commercial

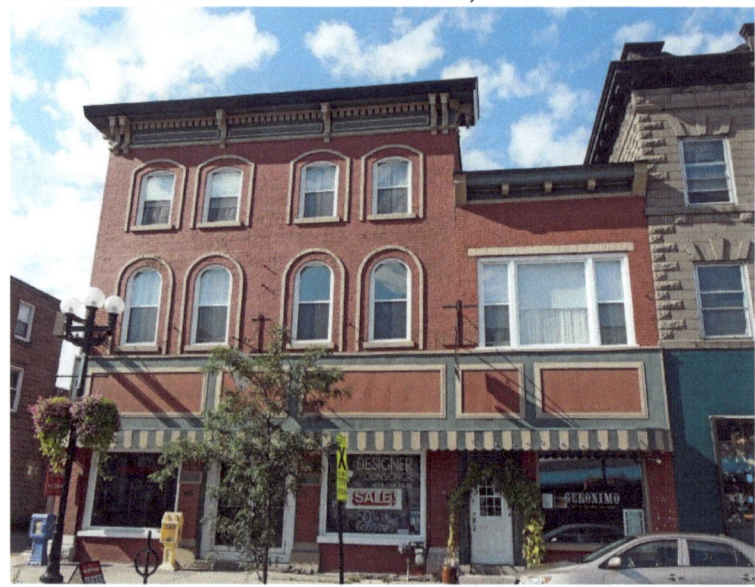

146-148 Prescott Street – in 1850 Thomas Baldwin had a cabinet shop here; after a fire it was rebuilt in 1872

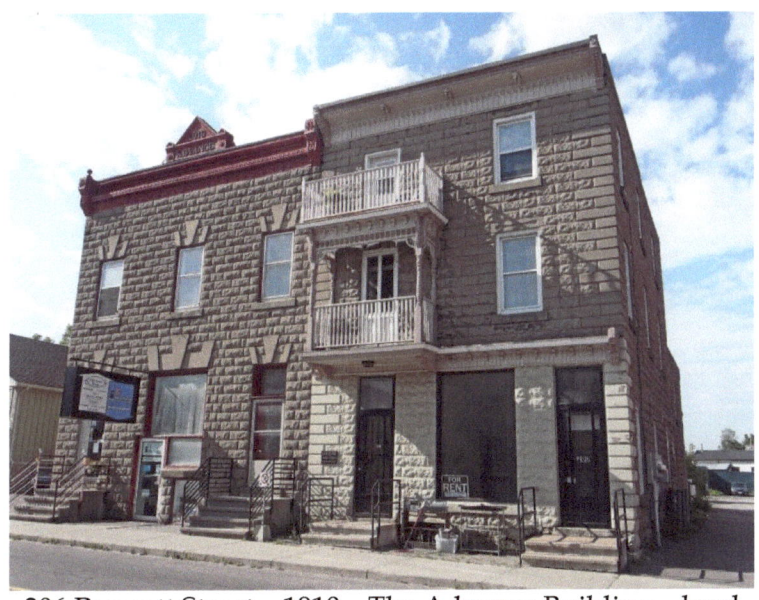

206 Prescott Street – 1910 – The Advance Building – local newspaper; 200-202 Prescott Street – George Tuck Block – 1902 – second and third floor balconies with decorative veranda supports, open railing

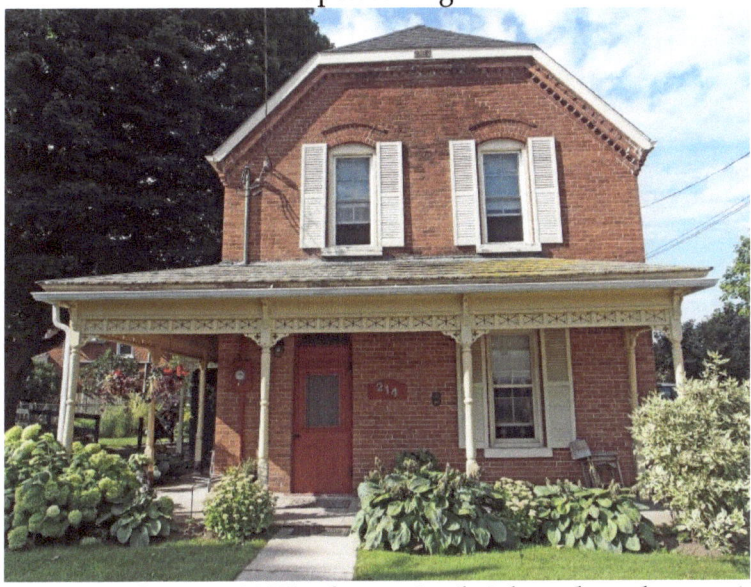

214 Prescott Street – 1897 – decorative brickwork under cornice; open wooden veranda with decorative railings and support posts

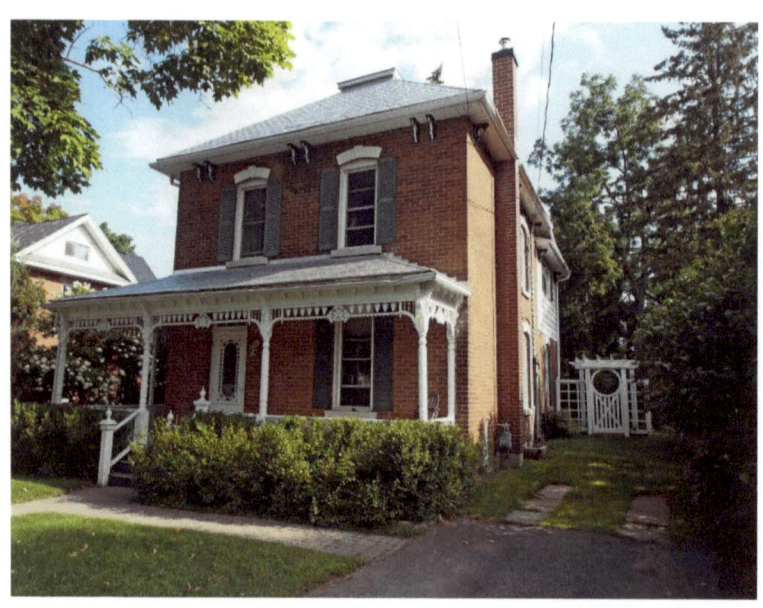

Prescott Street – Italianate - open wooden veranda with decorative support posts and open railings; hipped roof; paired cornice brackets; keystones above upper windows

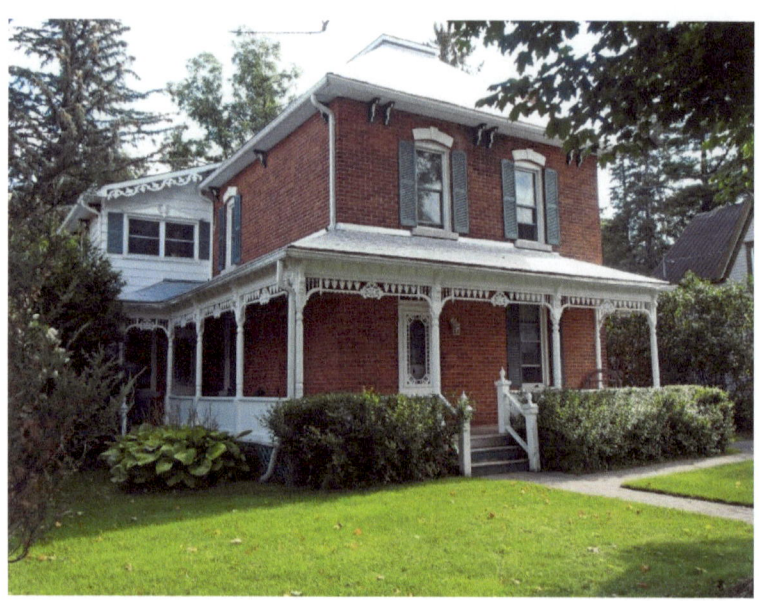

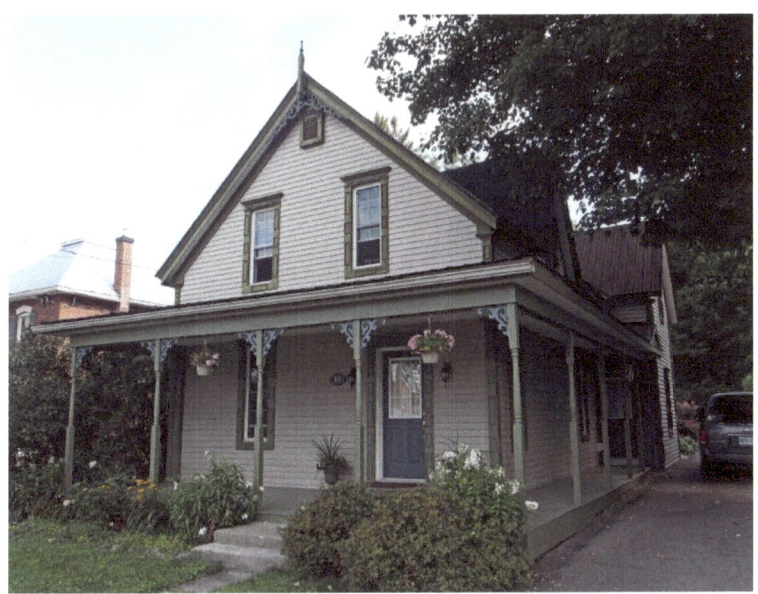

301 Prescott Street – Gothic – finial and verge board trim on gable, open wooden veranda with decorative support posts

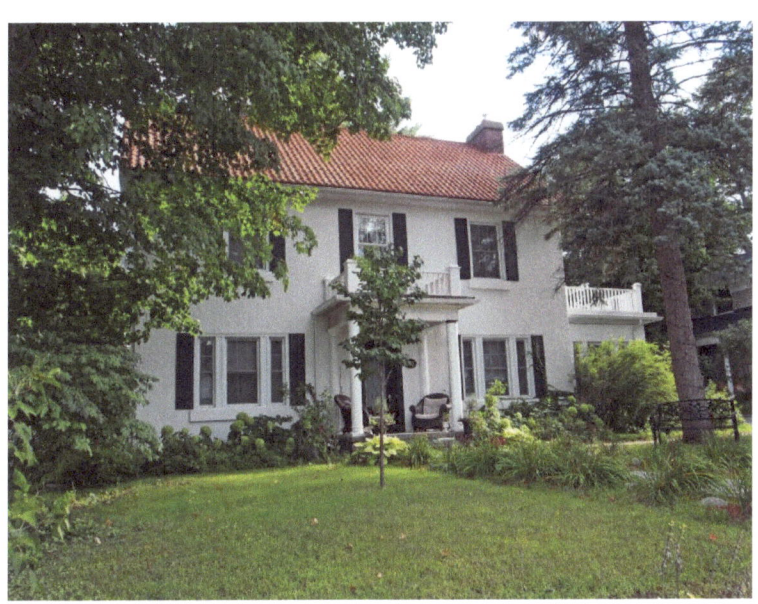

303 Prescott Street – round pillars supporting second floor balcony; second floor verandah on side

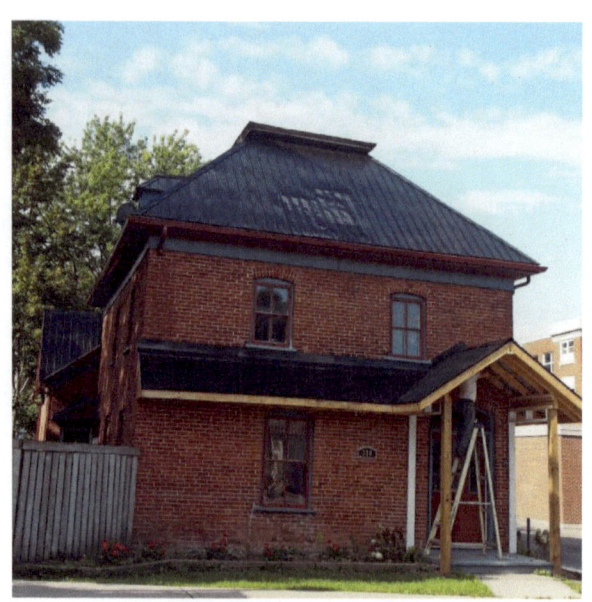

310 Prescott Street

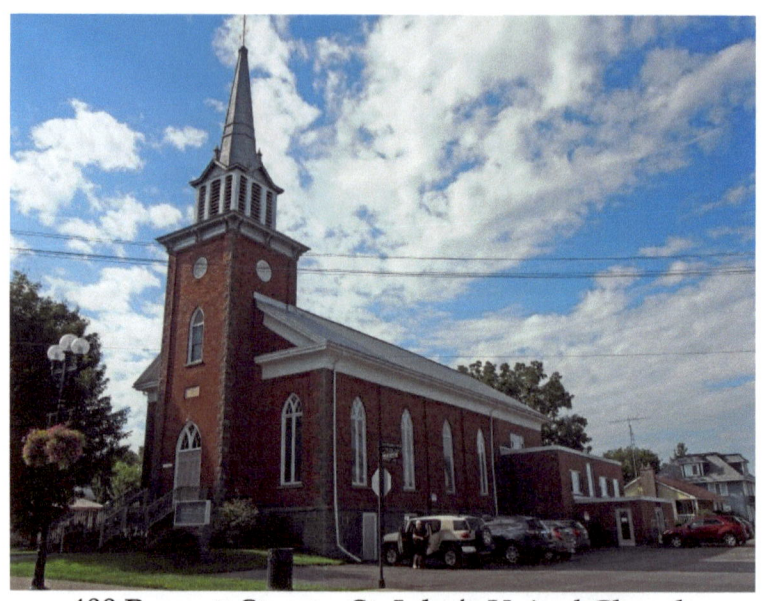

400 Prescott Street – St. John's United Church
(Wesleyan Methodist Church A.D. 1869)

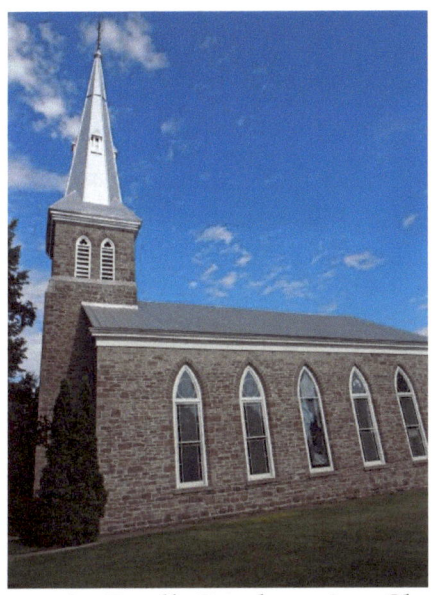

319 Prescott Street - St. Paul's Presbyterian Church – A.D. 1851

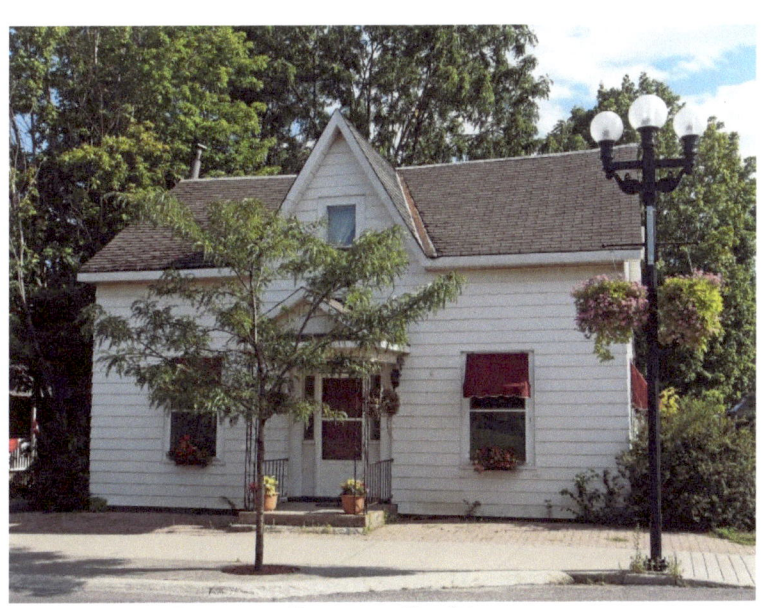

Prescott Street – Gothic cottage

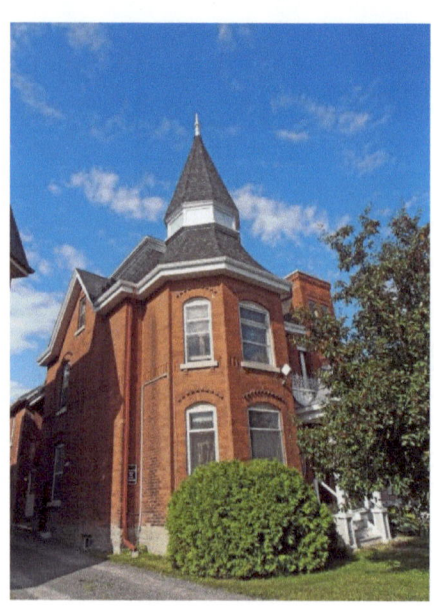

220-222 Prescott Street – de Pencier House – 1897- brick –
Queen Anne style – tower, turret, iron cresting

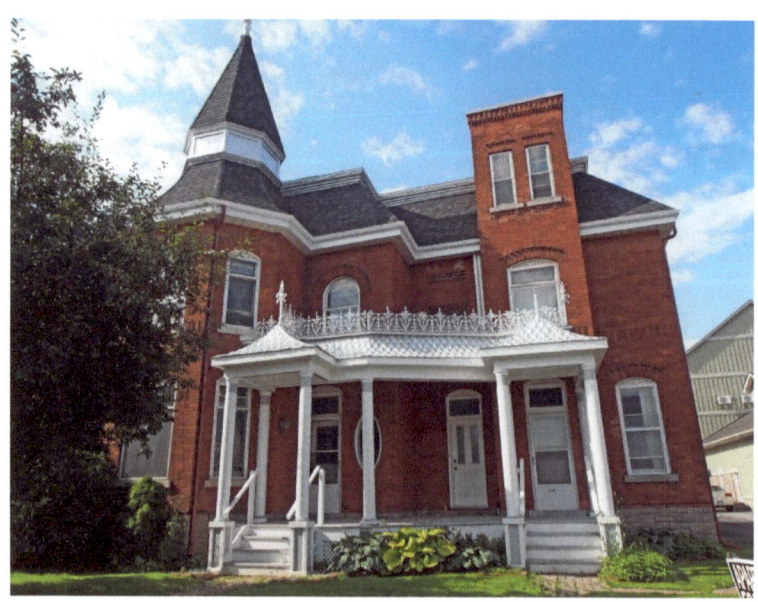

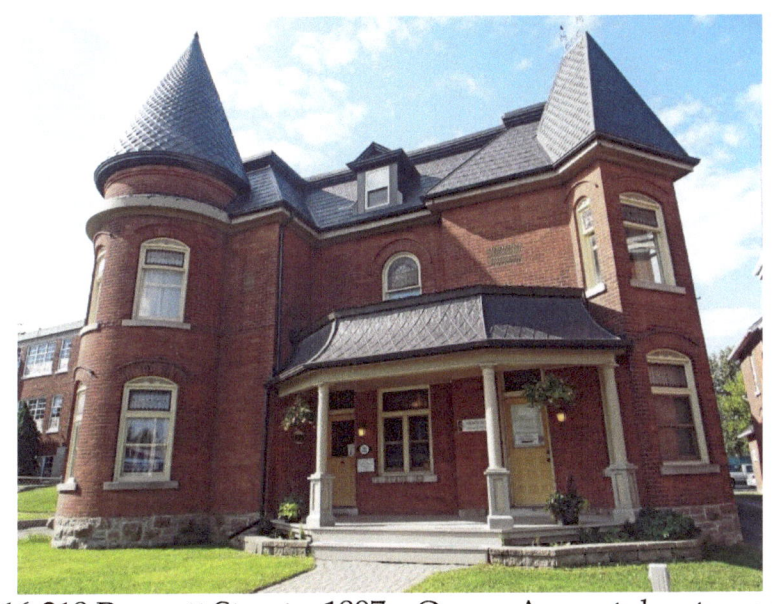

216-218 Prescott Street – 1897 – Queen Anne style – towers, dormer

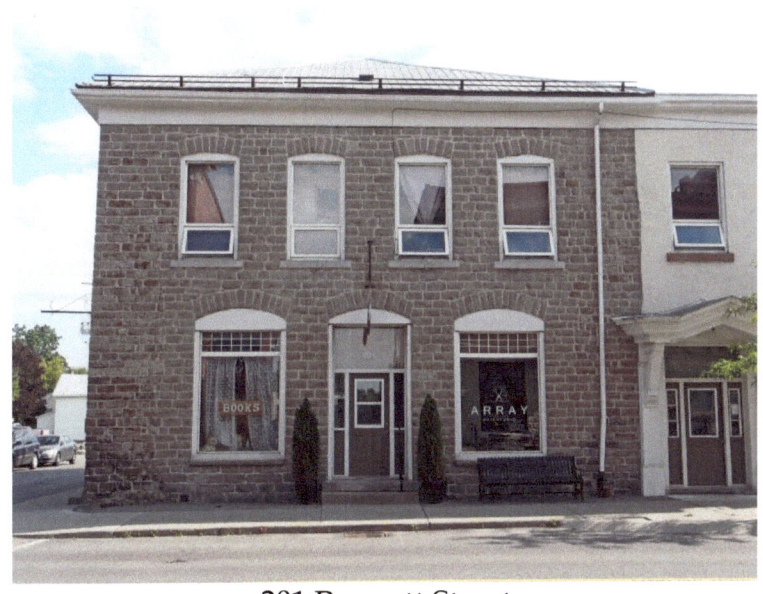

201 Prescott Street

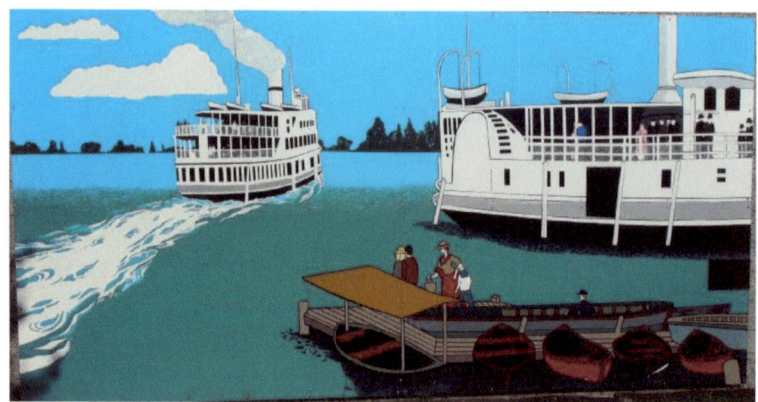

Mural

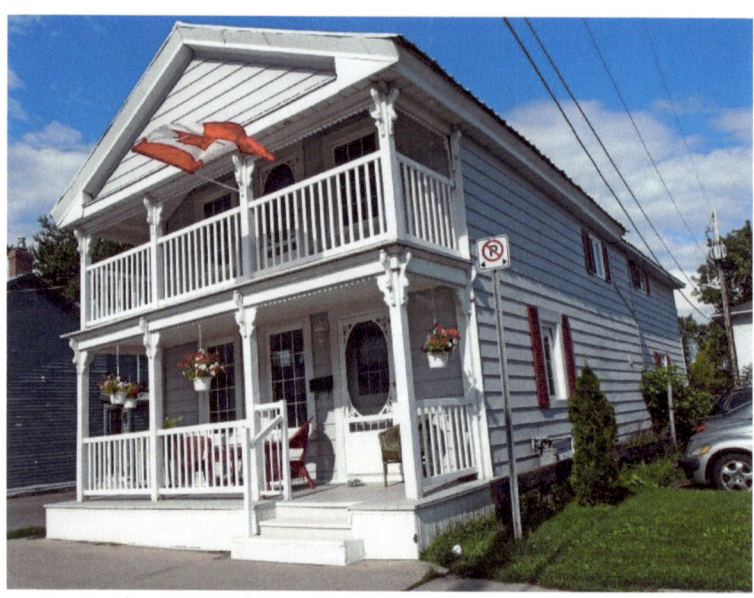

Open wooden verandas on both levels with decorative support posts and open railings

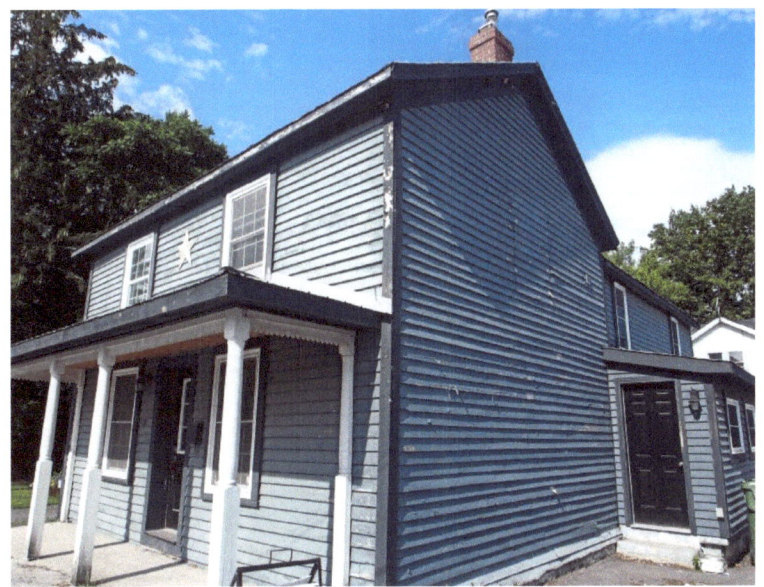

#15 – wood siding

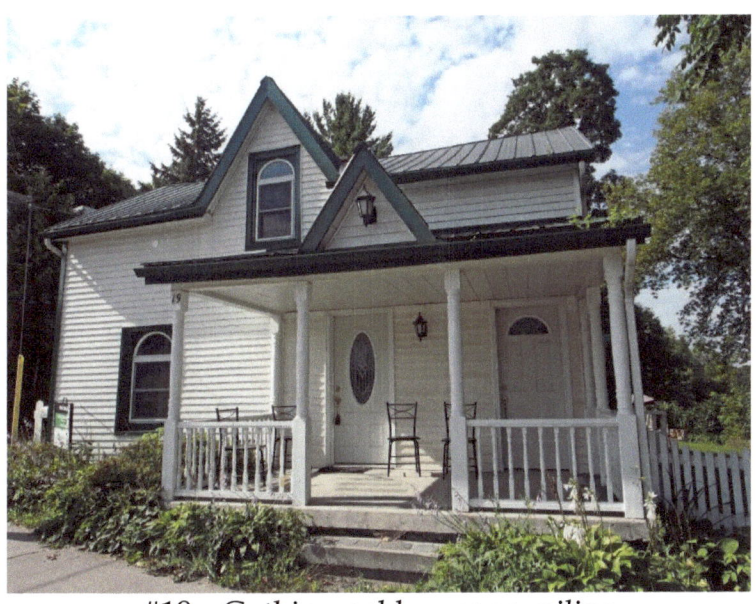

#19 – Gothic – gable – open railing

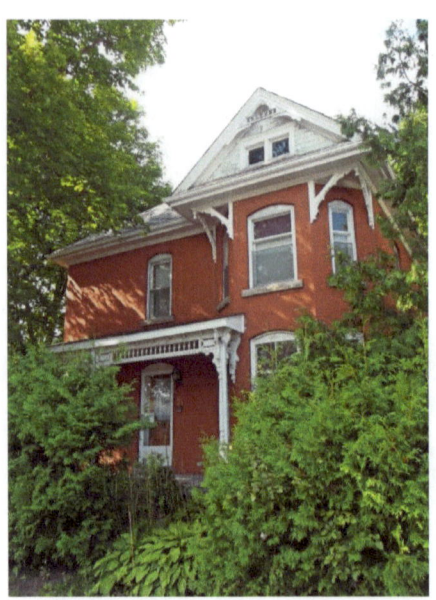

#21 – spindling on gable, fretwork, open wooden veranda with decorative support posts

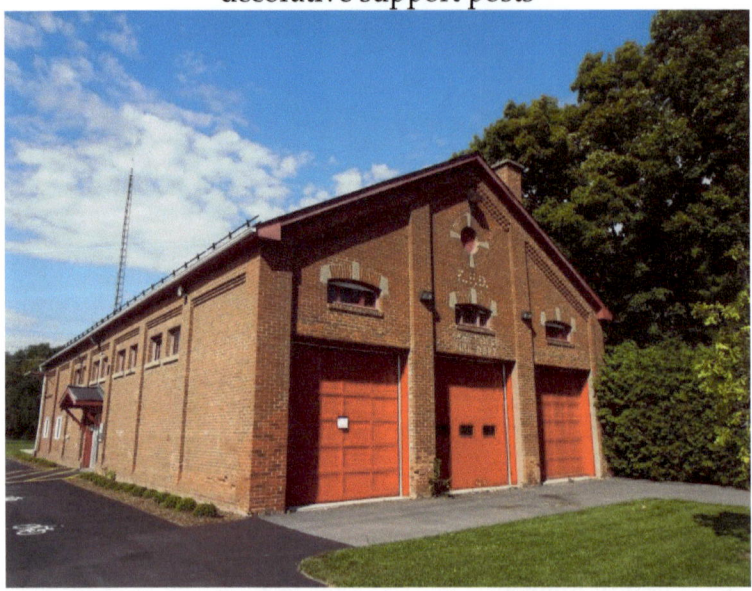

The first drill halls were built in Canada in the 1860s in response to the American Civil War and the Fenian raids. The Kemptville Armoury and Drill Hall was built in 1914 for use during World War I. The Fire Department used the building from 1968 to 2009. It is now home to the Kemptville Branch of the Navy League of Canada.

Forthton

Forthton Methodist Church - A.D. 1890 – Gothic – corner quoins,
lancet windows

Addison

Hipped roof, cornice brackets, corner quoins, pediment

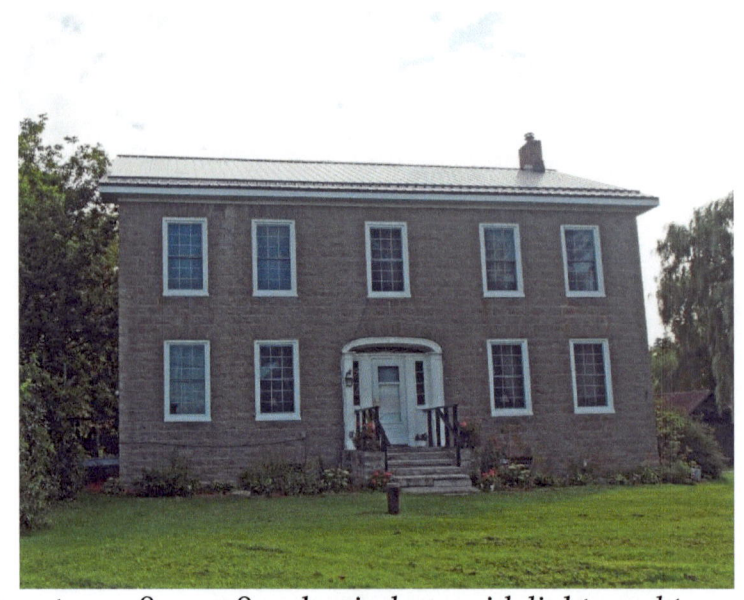

Limestone - 9-over-9 sash windows, sidelights and transom window

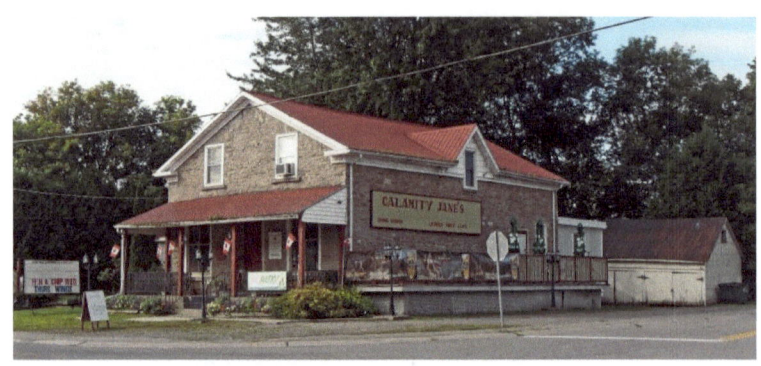

Calamity Jane's Dining Lounge, Addison – stone – Gothic – cornice return on gable

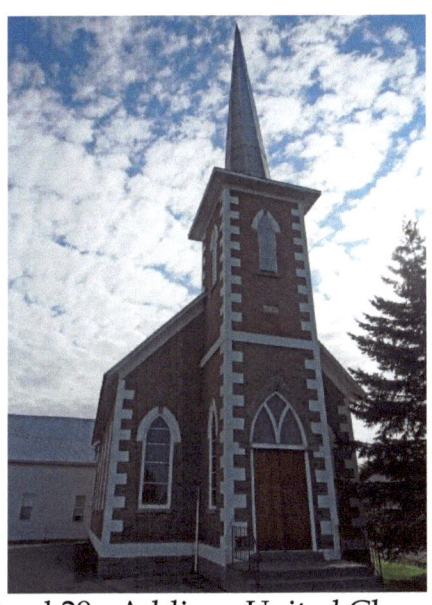

9007 County Road 29 - Addison United Church – A.D. 1891 -
The Episcopal Methodist built a church on the east side of
County Road 29 in the Village of Addison in 1881 of colored
red brick which was unusual at the time since most churches
of the period were constructed of stone.

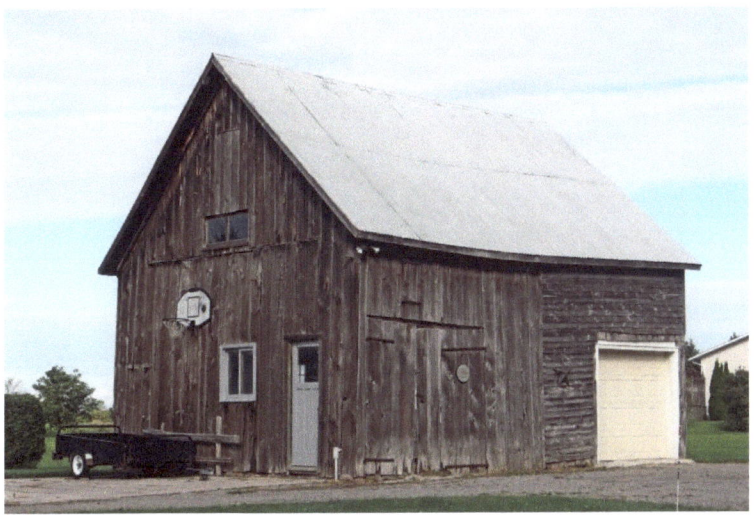

Toledo

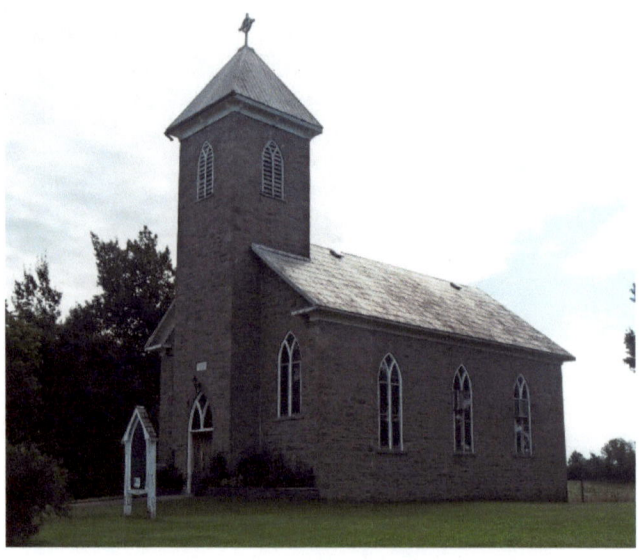

St. Thomas Church, Toledo – erected A.D. 1859 – Gothic, lancet windows

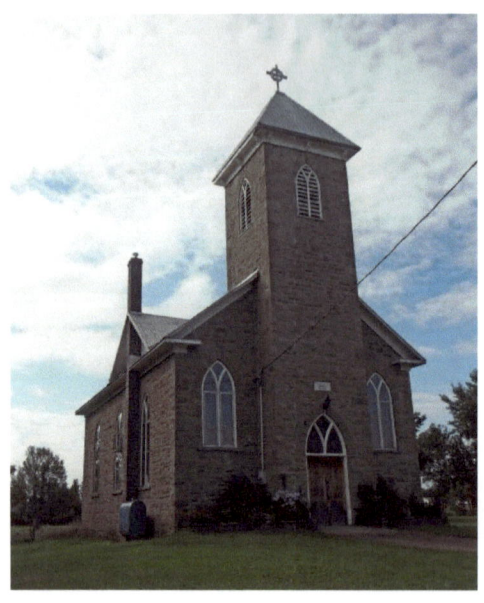

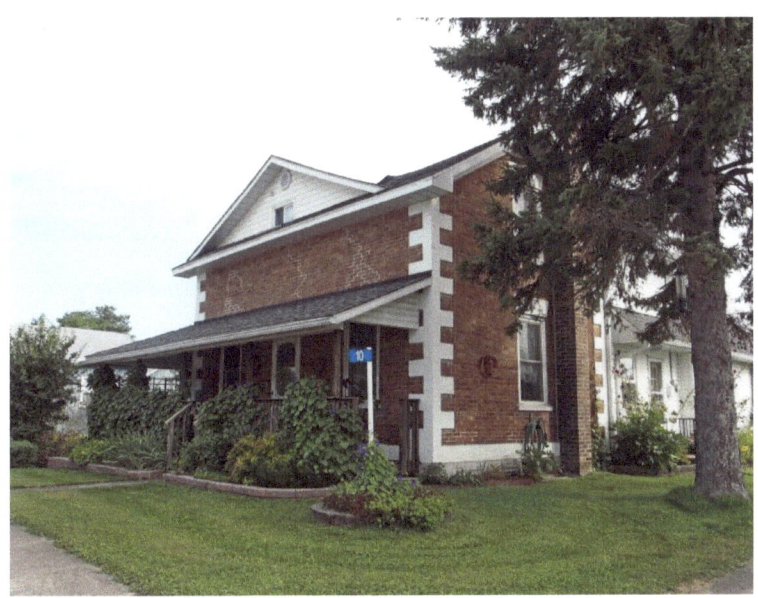

Corner quoins

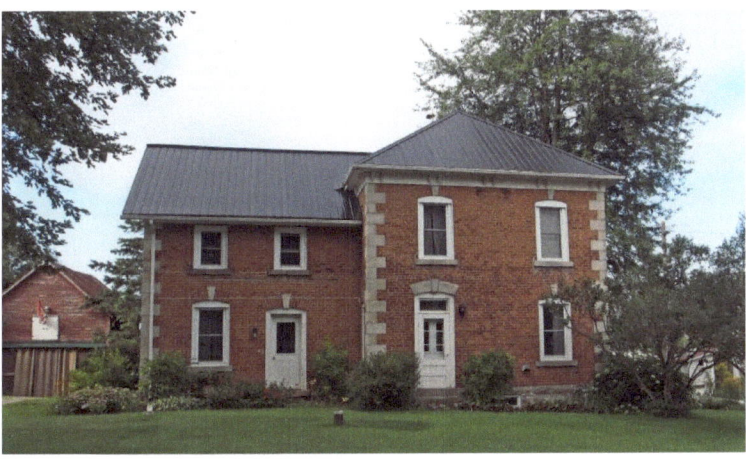

Corner quoins, hipped roof, voussoirs and keystones, cornice brackets

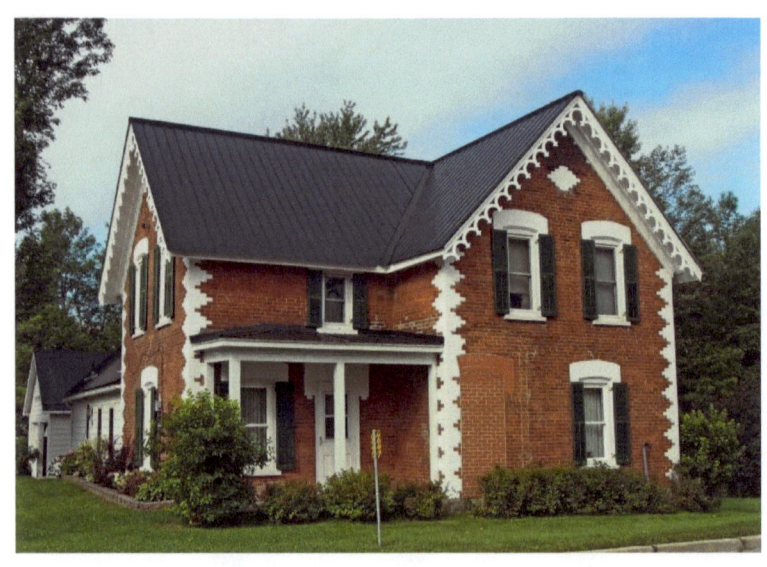

Gothic Revival – verge board trim on gables, painted corner quoins and voussoirs

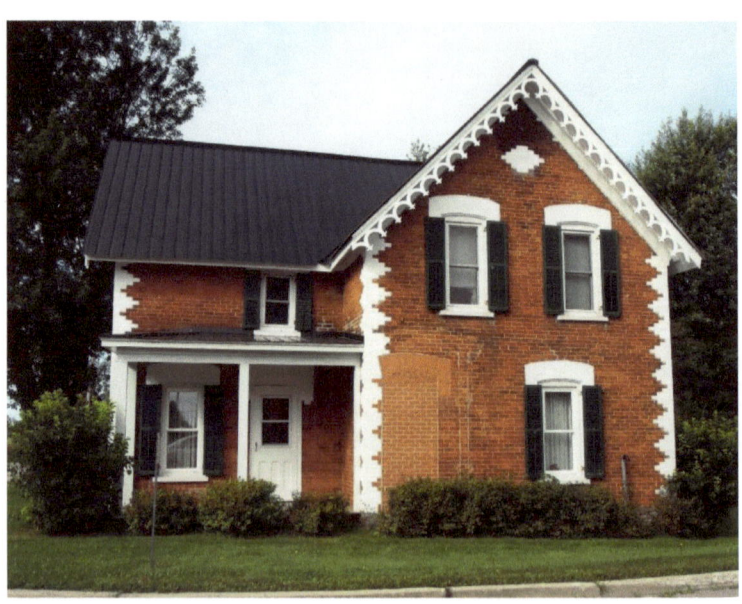

Newbliss

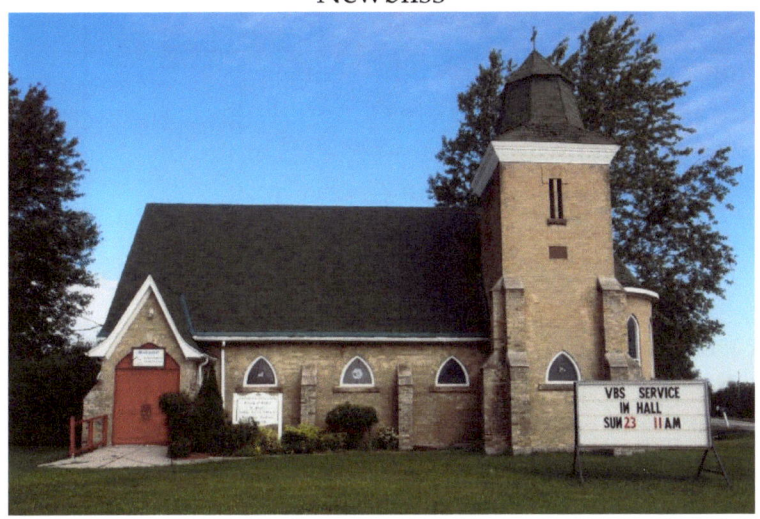

St. Paul's Anglican Church, Newbliss – Parish of Kitley
c. 1904 - Buttresses

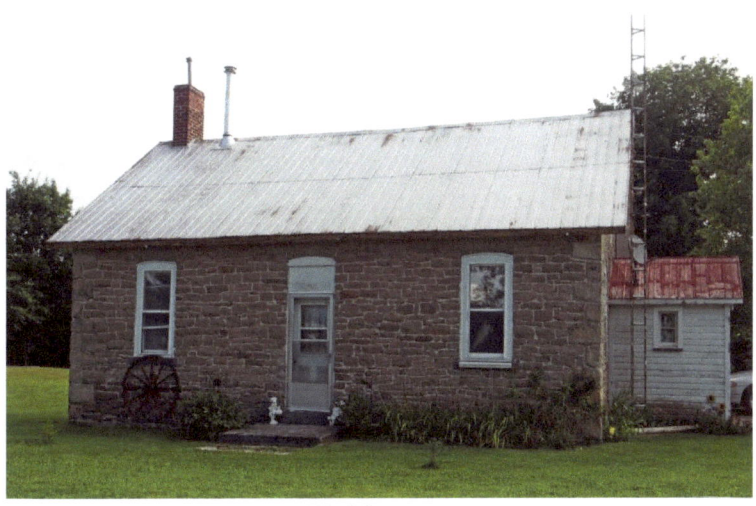

Field stone

Architectural Terms

Brackets: a decorative or weight-bearing structural element which forms a right angle with one side against a wall and the other under a projecting surface such as an eave or roof. Example: 126 Prescott Street, Page 19	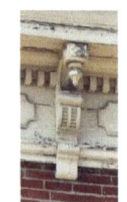
Buttress: a masonry structure built against or projecting from a wall which serves to support or reinforce the wall. In Canadian architecture, they are sometimes used for decoration. Example: 35 Clothier Street West, Page 8	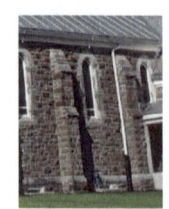
Cornice Return: decorative element on the end of a gable. Example: Calamity Jane's Dining Lounge, Addison, Page 32	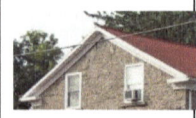
Dentil Moulding: an even series of rectangles used as ornamental decoration in cornices. Example: Prescott Street, Page 18	
Dichromatic brickwork: the use of two colours of brick, tile or slate to decorate a façade. Example: 11 Elizabeth Street, Page 16	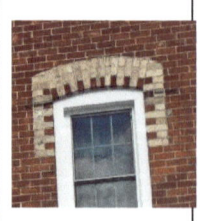

Dormer: (French for "sleep") a gable end window that pierces through the plane of a sloping roof surface to create usable space in the top floor or attic of a building by adding headroom. Example: 216-218 Prescott Street, Page 27	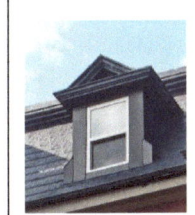
Fretwork: interlaced decorative design resembling a bracket Example: 104 Clothier Street East, Page 12	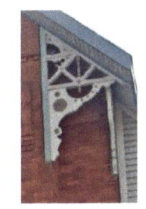
Gable: the triangular portion of a wall between the edges of a sloping roof. Example: 301 Prescott Street, Page 23	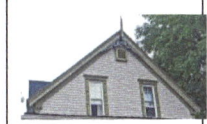
Hipped Roof: a roof where all sides slope downwards to the walls with no gables. Example: 5 Clothier Street West, Page 9	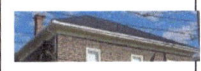
Iron Cresting: A decorative ornament along the top of a roof. Iron cresting was popular in the Baroque era and also in Italianate, Victorian, Second Empire and Queen Anne styles of architecture. Example: 220-222 Prescott Street, Page 26	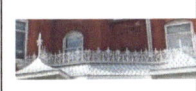

Keystones and Voussoirs: a voussoir is a wedge-shaped element used in building an arch. A keystone is the central stone that locks all the stones into position, allowing the arch to bear weight. A keystone is often enlarged and embellished. Example: 130-132 Prescott Street, Page 18	
Lancet Window: a tall, narrow window with a pointed arch at its top. Example: Forthton Methodist Church, Page 31	
Pediment: a triangular section above the door or portico, usually supported by columns. The inside of the triangle is called the tympanum. Example: Addison, Page 31	
Quoin: masonry blocks at the corner of a wall, often a decorative feature, usually larger or of a different colour than the rest of the wall. Example: Toledo, Page 35	

Rose Window: a circular window with ornamental tracery radiating from the centre. Example: 35 Clothier Street West, Page 8	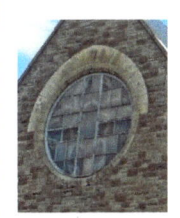
Sidelight: a vertical window that flanks a door, and is often used to emphasize the importance of a primary entrance. **Transom Window:** the light above the doorway, also called a fanlight. Example: Addison, Page 32	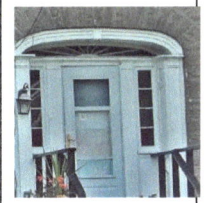
Tower: A circular, square, or octagonal vertical structure higher than the surrounding structure that is usually part of an existing building and is created either for extra defense or for a specific purpose such as a clock or a bell tower. Example: 216-218 Prescott Street, Page 27	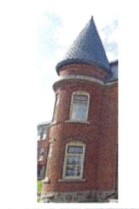
Turret: a small tower that projects from the wall of a building. Example: 220-222 Prescott Street, Page 26	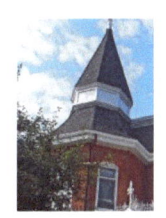
Verge board and Finial: also called bargeboards – hang from the projecting end of a roof and are often elaborately carved and ornamented. Example: Toledo, Page 36	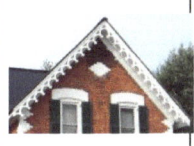

Gothic Revival, 1830-1890 – These decorative buildings have sharply-pitched gables with highly detailed verge boards, pointed-arch window openings, and dichromatic brickwork. It is a common style in Ontario. Example: St. Thomas Church, Toledo, Page 34	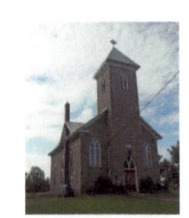
Italianate, 1850-1900 – A two story rectangular building with a mild hip roof, a projecting frontispiece, and generous eaves with ornate cornice brackets was the basis of the style; often there are large sash windows, quoins, ornate detailing on the windows, belvederes and wraparound verandahs. Example: Prescott Street, Page 22	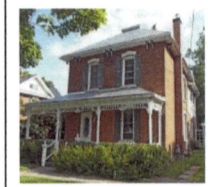
Queen Anne, 1885-1900 – This style is distinguished by an irregular outline featuring a combination of an offset tower, broad gables, projecting two-storey bays, verandahs, multi-sloped roofs, and tall, decorative chimneys. A mixture of brick and wood is common. Windows often have one large single-paned bottom sash and small panes in the upper sash. Example: 220-222 Prescott Street, Page 26	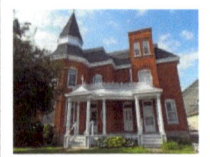
Regency Cottage, 1830-1860 – This style originated in England in 1815 and spread to Ontario later in the 19th century as British officers retired to Canada. It is a modest one-storey house with a low-pitched hip roof and has a symmetrical front façade. Example: 12 Elizabeth Street, Page 16	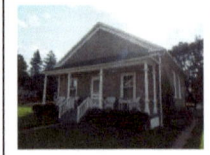

www.ingramcontent.com/pod-product-compliance
Lightning Source LLC
Chambersburg PA
CBHW040928180526
45159CB00002BA/661